GUINNESS WORLD RECORDS

RECORD-BREAKING COMPREHENSION

YEAR

6

Alison Milford

Published by

RISING ★ STARS

in association with

Rising Stars UK Ltd.
7 Hatchers Mews, Bermondsey Street, London, SE1 3GS
www.risingstars-uk.com

Published 2013

Published in association with Guinness World Records.

Author: Alison Milford
Text design: Burville-Riley Partnership/Fakenham Prepress Solutions
Logo design: Words & Pictures Ltd
Typesetting: Fakenham Prepress Solutions
Cover design: Burville-Riley Partnership
Publisher: Becca Law
Project manager: Tracey Cowell
Editor: Jennie Clifford

Photo acknowledgements
Page 10: © phototropic/iStockphoto; **page 12**: © Kazuhiko Yoshino/iStockphoto, fuzzimo; **page 22**: © PHOTOgraphica/iStockphoto, fuzzimo; **page 26**: © Chunumunu/iStockphoto; **page 28**: © Alexander Kazantsev/iStockphoto; **page 34**: © chrisdeana/iStockphoto; **page 48**: © AlexKV/iStockphoto; **page 54**: © small_frog/iStockphoto. **Rising Stars is grateful to Guinness World Records for supplying all of the record-related pictures in the book**.

British Library Cataloguing in Publication Data.
A CIP record for this book is available from the British Library.

ISBN: 978-0-85769-566-6

Printed by Craft Print International Limited, Singapore

CONTENTS

How to use this book   4

Reading comprehension   6
Reading between the lines   7

Most buildings climbed unassisted   8
Longest motorcycle ride through a tunnel of fire   10
Most expensive fungus species   12
Largest tug-of-war tournament   14
Largest revolving restaurant   16
Longest full-body-contact ice endurance   18
Youngest film director   20
Most tattooed person   22
Longest theatrical run   24
Most pots thrown in one hour by an individual   26
Longest rail grind on a snowboard   28
Greatest distance covered in 24 hours by wheelchair   30
Largest gathering of people dressed as Mohandas Gandhi   32
First gorilla born in captivity   34
Largest matchstick model   36
Largest violin   38
Largest concentration of geysers   40
Largest photo mosaic   42
Most consecutive foot-juggling flips   44
Largest panoramic painting   46
Longest time to live with a bullet in the head   48
Longest distance run full-body burn (without oxygen)   50
Oldest sculpture   52
Largest medicinal herb garden   54

Reading skills   56

HOW TO USE THIS BOOK

Record-Breaking Comprehension features some of the most fascinating, weird and wonderful records from the Guinness World Records archive.

In this book, you will:

- read the exciting record-breaking stories
- practise and improve your comprehension skills
- go beyond the record to find out more.

The text

Each record or topic is described using a fiction or non-fiction text type, including newspaper reports, instructional web pages, blog entries and letters.

RECORD-BREAKING COMPREHENSION

MOST BUILDINGS CLIMBED UNASSISTED

14   **Sydney Express**   Tuesday 10 August 2010

Letters

We have received numerous letters about Alain Robert. Alain is a solo urban climber from France, who holds the Guinness World Record for most buildings climbed unassisted. Following his climb in Sydney yesterday, Alain has now climbed 100 towers, monuments and skyscrapers. His most notable achievements include reaching the top of the Petronas Towers in Kuala Lumpur, Malaysia in 2009, and climbing to the top of Burj Khalifa tower (tallest building in the world) in Dubai, UAE in 2011.

Spiderman triumphs

Dear Editor

Yesterday, I witnessed Alain 'Spiderman' Robert's incredible 57-storey building climb. His sheer courage was awe-inspiring, especially as he suffers from vertigo.

I know that Alain doesn't use ropes or suction devices for his climbs but I knew he wouldn't fall. He was steady, and quickly and confidently used pipes and window frames to help him scale the building.

From what I can tell, many agree that Alain Robert is a real superhero! I found out that he helps raise awareness and funds for good causes. I feel so lucky to have seen him. Keep climbing, 'Spiderman'!

Melina Faro, Sydney

8

Questions

Answer the questions to help you practise and improve your reading comprehension skills.

For help on answering questions, see pages 6–7.

The questions cover a range of different reading skills. For more information on these skills, see page 56.

Most buildings climbed unassisted

ON YOUR MARKS

a. What country does Alain come from?
b. Does Melina write using formal or informal language? Give examples.
c. How does Melina feel about Alain Robert?
d. How would you feel if you watched Alain climb a tall building? Why?

GET SET

a. What does Alain use to help him climb buildings?
b. How could vertigo be a problem for Alain?
c. Why might Melina feel 'lucky' to have seen Alain?
d. Do you think Alain is brave? Give reasons.

Beyond the record

In this section you will be asked to find out more about a record or topic and present your findings. This might be by using books or the internet.

GO FOR GOLD!

a. Write down two adverbs used in the text.
b. Why does Alain Robert have the nickname 'Spiderman'?
c. What does 'solo urban climber' mean?
d. Why do you think Alain climbs buildings unsupported?

BEYOND THE RECORD

Use the internet to find out more about Alain 'Spiderman' Robert. Choose one of his record-breaking climbs and create a newspaper front-page report. Include a powerful headline, the who, what, why, when and where, and also reported and direct speech.

9

READING COMPREHENSION

Reading the text

Read the text carefully. Don't rush. Try to immerse yourself in the information and enjoy it.

When you have finished, take a moment to reflect and think about what you have read. What was the author's purpose? Did the text make sense? Was there anything you didn't understand?

The questions

Always read the questions carefully before you begin to write. Then you will understand what you are being asked to do.

The questions check that you can:

- make sense of what you are reading
- find information and ideas in the text
- work out what the author means
- understand why a text is organised in a particular way
- comment on vocabulary and style
- say how a text makes you feel
- link what you read to your own life.

Answering the questions

Read the instructions carefully before you start to answer, as they give you information about how to answer the questions. Don't rush your answer.

Remember to refer to the text. You do not need to answer any questions from memory.

READING BETWEEN THE LINES

An author doesn't always tell you exactly what is happening. He or she often gives you clues to help you work it out for yourself.

Read the text below and then look at the worked question examples underneath.

> Woofs and wags abounded at the annual Summer Fair. There were 15 entrants who competed for the Toss and Fetch Cup. This was won by Andy May and Buster. Buster caught one disc as many times as Andy could throw it in 60 seconds. He gained extra points by making several mid-air catches and was awarded a respectable 9.5 points.
>
> Another duo, Misty and Olivia, hope to go on to international competitions.
>
> 'We are practising hard to get Misty holding more discs and want to try for the Guinness World Record,' said proud owner Olivia.

a. How many entrants were in the competition?

The answer can be found in the text itself – 15.

b. What or who is Buster?

The text doesn't actually say, but from reading the clues ('Woofs and wags', 'Toss and Fetch Cup') it becomes clear that Buster is a dog.

c. How did Misty's owner feel about her dog's success?

Again, the text doesn't actually say, but you can draw your own conclusion from the text: '"We are practising hard to get Misty holding more discs and want to try for the Guinness World Record," said proud owner Olivia' implies that Olivia is very pleased with Misty's success.

14

Sydney Express Tuesday 10 August 2010

Letters

We have received numerous letters about Alain Robert. Alain is a solo urban climber from France, who holds the Guinness World Record for most buildings climbed unassisted. Following his climb in Sydney yesterday, Alain has now climbed 100 towers, monuments and skyscrapers. His most notable achievements include reaching the top of the Petronas Towers in Kuala Lumpur, Malaysia in 2009, and climbing to the top of Burj Khalifa tower (tallest building in the world) in Dubai, UAE in 2011.

Spiderman triumphs

Dear Editor

Yesterday, I witnessed Alain 'Spiderman' Robert's incredible 57-storey building climb. His sheer courage was awe-inspiring, especially as he suffers from vertigo.

I know that Alain doesn't use ropes or suction devices for his climbs but I knew he wouldn't fall. He was steady, and quickly and confidently used pipes and window frames to help him scale the building.

From what I can tell, many agree that Alain Robert is a real superhero! I found out that he helps raise awareness and funds for good causes. I feel so lucky to have seen him. Keep climbing, 'Spiderman'!

Melina Faro, Sydney

ON YOUR MARKS

a. What country does Alain come from?

b. Does Melina write using formal or informal language? Give examples.

c. How does Melina feel about Alain Robert?

d. How would you feel if you watched Alain climb a tall building? Why?

GET SET

a. What does Alain use to help him climb buildings?

b. How could vertigo be a problem for Alain?

c. Why might Melina feel 'lucky' to have seen Alain?

d. Do you think Alain is brave? Give reasons.

GO FOR GOLD!

a. Write down two adverbs used in the text.

b. Why does Alain Robert have the nickname 'Spiderman'?

c. What does 'solo urban climber' mean?

d. Why do you think Alain climbs buildings unsupported?

BEYOND THE RECORD

Use the internet to find out more about Alain 'Spiderman' Robert. Choose one of his record-breaking climbs and create a newspaper front-page report. Include a powerful headline, the who, what, why, when and where, and also reported and direct speech.

LONGEST MOTORCYCLE RIDE THROUGH A TUNNEL OF FIRE

SAFETY NOTICE
DO NOT TRY THIS AT HOME!

Subtitle script
Show: *Guinness World Records – Ab Indian Todega*
Date: 13 March 2011

HANSA: Welcome to *Guinness World Records – Ab Indian Todega*: the show that brings you the most wacky, extraordinary and daring Guinness World Record attempts.

'Daring' is exactly how I would describe our first record attempt: the longest motorcycle ride through a tunnel of fire.

What makes this attempt all the more remarkable is that the driver is our very own Shabir Ahluwalia!

I have just been told that Shabir is ready to go. Over to you, Shilpa.

SHILPA: We're outside the studio and just moments away from Shabir's death-defying attempt. There is a real sense of tension in the air.

Shabir is wearing anti-inflammable clothing and a special mask under his crash helmet.

There's the signal! The 68.49 m wood tunnel has been lit. The heat is intense!

Shabir is racing at full speed down the runway towards the blazing tunnel. That bike is incredibly powerful. And he's in! Huge flames are spurting out everywhere. This is such a hazardous feat but Shabir seems utterly fearless!

And he's out! Shabir has done it! The medics are checking him now and – yes, he's OK! Back to you, Hansa.

ON YOUR MARKS

a. What three adjectives are used by Hansa to describe the Guinness World Record attempts that you might see on the show?

b. Why did Shabir wear a special mask under his crash helmet?

c. Why did Shabir's motorbike need to be powerful?

d. Do you think Shabir was scared during the record attempt? Why?

GET SET

a. Find and write down two descriptive words that mean 'dangerous'.

b. Why would there be 'a real sense of tension'?

c. Why would this record attempt need strict safety rules?

d. How would your opinion change about Shabir as a presenter of the show after the record attempt?

GO FOR GOLD!

a. Write down the phrase that describes Shabir during the attempt.

b. Why was Shabir's attempt described as 'death-defying'?

c. Why do you think Shabir was 'racing at full speed'?

d. Why do you think such a dangerous record attempt was shown on television?

BEYOND THE RECORD

On 10 August 2012 the Guinness World Record for the longest motorcycle ride through a tunnel of fire was broken by Andre De Kock and Enrico Schoeman in Vaalwater, Limpopo Province, South Africa. They rode a motorcycle and sidecar combination through a 103.09-m tunnel. Imagine that you are a TV presenter reporting on this record attempt. Write a short script about what you see. What language will you use to convey interesting information, excitement and tension?

11

MOST EXPENSIVE FUNGUS SPECIES

Notes for white truffle presentation

**Bigsby Village Hall,
Wednesday 12th September,
7.00 pm**

In this short presentation, I am going to introduce you to a fascinating species of fungus: the white truffle. A fungus is an organism that grows in damp conditions. Different types of fungi include mushrooms, mould and yeast.

Like some mushrooms, the white truffle can be eaten but it costs a vast amount of money. In fact, it holds the Guinness World Record for the most expensive fungus species, costing up to £3,000 per kg. To put that into perspective, white mushrooms only cost about £4.00 per kg!

There are several reasons why the white truffle is so expensive.

- First, it is extremely rare. It can only be found in the Italian regions of Tuscany, Piedmont, Emilia-Romagna and Marches, and the Istrian Peninsula of Croatia.
- Second, it is very hard to find because it grows to a depth of 30.5 cm underground. Luckily, the white truffle has a distinct odour, which dogs and pigs can smell even under layers of soil. As a result, these animals are sometimes trained as 'truffle hogs' to sniff and dig out the round-shaped truffles.
- Third, the white truffle is seen as a food delicacy. Often referred to as the 'diamond of the table', it is so precious that some chefs have been known to lock white truffles in a safe overnight!

So, how do you eat the white truffle? Because it has a very strong smell and taste, it is usually gently grated onto dishes such as risottos, pasta and mashed potatoes.

To conclude, the white truffle is one of the most intriguing species of fungus in the world. It grows in hard-to-find places, looks odd and smells quite revolting, but it is highly prized all over the world. I would love to find one!

Thank you so much for listening to my presentation. I hope this sparks your interest in the subject. Does anyone have any questions?

ON YOUR MARKS

a. In what sort of conditions do fungi grow?
b. Why might some chefs lock white truffles in a safe?
c. Why do you think that only dogs and pigs can smell white truffles?
d. Which part of the presentation did you find most interesting? Why?

GET SET

a. Why is a white truffle called the 'diamond of the table'?
b. Why do you think dogs and pigs have to be 'trained' to find white truffles?
c. Why is there an exclamation mark after the sentence about the price of white mushrooms?
d. Do you think white truffles offer value for money? Why?

GO FOR GOLD!

a. What are the three reasons why white truffles are so expensive?
b. What does 'food delicacy' mean?
c. Why do you think chefs would only want to 'gently grate' a white truffle onto food?
d. Which part of the presentation do you think needs more information? Why?

BEYOND THE RECORD

Imagine you have just seen the white truffle presentation. Write down five questions to ask the presenter. Think carefully about the words you use. Use the text to find examples of truffle-related vocabulary.

LARGEST TUG-OF-WAR TOURNAMENT

www.encyclopaedia-file.com/tug-of-war

Tug of war

Tug of war is a sport of strength in which two teams of people grasp opposite ends of a long rope and try to pull their opponents over a central line.

History

Although historians are unsure when tug of war began, there is evidence to suggest many ancient cultures used it for ceremonial rituals, as a strengthening exercise or as a competitive game.

In Ancient China, tug of war was often used to train warriors for battle. It was also very popular as a game in which teams of up to 500 people would compete against each other.

In Ancient Greece, tug-of-war sports teams competed against each other in the Olympics.

Viking warriors would pull on either end of an animal skin over an open fire to test their heroic qualities. Tug of war was also played in medieval tournaments and by sailors on board their ships.

Between 1900 and 1920, competitive tug-of-war events were held in the Olympic Games but the event was eventually dropped because the organisers saw it as a game, rather than a sport.

Present day

Today, tug of war is played all over the world, either as a proper sport or as a friendly game between teams at local fairs or on sports days.

On 17 November 2010, students from Het Nieuwe Lyceum and De Werkplaats in the Netherlands broke the record for the world's largest tug-of-war tournament. The tournament was held at Het Nieuwe Lyceum, where the 1,290 competitors were split into three team categories: junior students, senior students and adults.

ON YOUR MARKS

a. What record did the students from the Netherlands break?
b. What does 'grasp' mean?
c. Why would tug of war have been played by sailors?
d. Write down three qualities you think are important for a tug-of-war team member.

GET SET

a. What did Viking warriors use in tug of war instead of rope?
b. What 'heroic qualities' do you think Viking warriors were testing?
c. Why is the definition of 'tug of war' given at the beginning of the text?
d. Why do you think tug of war has lasted for thousands of years?

GO FOR GOLD!

a. Name three ways in which ancient cultures used tug of war.
b. Why do you think tug of war is a good 'strengthening exercise'?
c. What is the difference between tug of war as a game and as a sport?
d. Do you think the Olympic organisers were right not to continue to include tug of war in the Olympic Games? Why?

BEYOND THE RECORD

Use the internet to find out the official rules of tug of war. Present this information as an easy-to-follow set of instructions aimed at someone who wants to take up the sport. Use bullet points, formal language, imperative verbs and sub-headings.

LARGEST REVOLVING RESTAURANT

Eating Out

Bellini

"*Stunning views, scrumptious food*" 9/10

It is early evening. My companion and I chat excitedly as we walk into the Mexico City World Trade Center, passing office workers keen to get home for their dinner. We are also looking forward to our meal, so we get into the lift and press the button for the 45th floor.

When the doors open, we are confronted with a huge, airy, circular restaurant with large windows offering stunning panoramic views over Mexico City. We have arrived at Bellini, the largest revolving restaurant in the world. Opened in 1994, the restaurant covers an area of 1,044.66 m^2 and seats 332 people.

Although its size could make it overwhelming, this simply isn't the case. The thoughtful seating and the circular plan of the restaurant is welcoming to diners. You can choose to sit by one of the bars, at small square tables or in more private semi-circular booths.

However, it gets even better. The dining and bar areas are **all** on a revolving platform that moves so slowly that it takes 1 hour, 45 minutes to rotate a full circle. You have a guaranteed 360° view as you enjoy your meal – and you don't feel dizzy!

A waiter guides us to the bar area, for a pre-meal drink and a chance to look at the menu. As the setting sun casts a gorgeous reddish glow across the city, and as street lights twinkle, Bellini is filled with the aroma of delicious traditional Mexican food, laughing families and romantic couples. Bellini is truly a *head-turning* experience!

Paulino Romero

25

ON YOUR MARKS

a. Where is Bellini located?

b. Why is the word 'all' in bold?

c. What kind of mood is the writer in as she is on her way to the restaurant?

d. Which part of the restaurant do you think sounds the most impressive? Why?

GET SET

a. Find and write down the sentence that explains why you don't feel dizzy in Bellini.

b. Why has the writer added an exclamation mark after 'and you don't feel dizzy'?

c. Why do you think 'head-turning' is written in italics?

d. Does the review make you want to visit the restaurant? Why?

GO FOR GOLD!

a. Write down three powerful adjectives the writer uses to describe the restaurant.

b. How does the writer conjure up the atmosphere of Bellini in the last paragraph?

c. How does the writer initially feel when she arrives at Bellini? How does this feeling change?

d. Do you think the review covers everything about the restaurant? What would you also include?

BEYOND THE RECORD

Plan and write a review of a restaurant. Use a thesaurus to list powerful verbs and descriptive adjectives that could be included in the review.

LONGEST FULL-BODY-CONTACT ICE ENDURANCE

| Home | Biography | Current projects | Activities | Contact |

Iceman

Wim Hof was born on 20 April 1959 in the Netherlands. He is known as the 'Iceman' due to his astonishing ability to remain unaffected by the extreme cold.

From an early age, Wim loved the cold. He often runs barefoot across freezing snow. Over the years, he has rigorously trained his body, using meditation and exercise to prepare for ice-endurance world record attempts.

How does he do it?

Until recently, Wim's remarkable abilities had left many scientists baffled. However, while testing how his body would react in a tank of ice, the scientists made an amazing discovery. During deep meditation, Wim's brain sent messages to other parts of his body, telling them to stay warm. Experts say this is highly unusual. For any other person, their body temperature would drop dangerously low, resulting in possible death. Despite this, Wim believes that most people can control their body temperature just by concentrating hard.

Breaking records

Wim has set three different Guinness World Records and broken them several times. One of his most memorable attempts was on 17 November 2011, when he broke the record for the longest time spent in direct, full-body contact with ice. He achieved this by sitting in a tank up to his neck in ice for 1 hour, 52 minutes, 42 seconds. The record attempt was filmed and broadcast on the TV programme *Fox & Friends*, in New York, USA.

The Iceman's other chilly achievements

❋ Running a full marathon (26 miles) in temperatures of −20°C, in a pair of shorts.
❋ Swimming 66 m under ice, wearing just shorts and goggles.
❋ Climbing high, icy mountains, in just a pair of shorts.

ON YOUR MARKS

a. Why is Wim Hof called the 'Iceman'?
b. How does running 'barefoot across freezing snow' show that Wim is different to most people?
c. How do the sub-headings in the web page help the reader?
d. How would you feel if you saw Wim sitting in a tank of ice?

GET SET

a. How does Wim train his body to cope with the extreme cold?
b. Why do you think scientists were baffled by Wim's abilities?
c. Why are 'The Iceman's other chilly achievements' in a bulleted list at the end of the web page?
d. Wim Hof is unique in what he can do. Why would you not advise others to copy him?

GO FOR GOLD!

a. Why is it dangerous for most people to experience extreme cold?
b. What does 'meditation' mean?
c. Why do you think Wim only wears shorts when he is doing his endurance tests?
d. Do you agree with Wim's view that people can control their body temperature through meditation? Give reasons for your answer.

BEYOND THE RECORD

Imagine that Wim Hof is planning to visit your school to talk about his ideas and achievements. Write a list of eight questions you would like to ask him.

Mumbai Film Review • March 2006

Care of Footpath

Director: Kishan Shrikanth

Lead actors: Jackie Shroff, Saurabh Shukla, Thaara, Kishan

When the international film community heard that a nine-year-old Indian film star was directing his first movie, many thought it would be a childish and amateurish affair. How wrong they were.

Care of Footpath is a triumph. Not only is it beautifully acted and technically stunning, but it is also immensely inspiring, thanks to the incredible talent of its young director, writer and star, Kishan Shrikanth.

Born on 6 January 1996, Kishan started acting at the age of four and, by 2006, had appeared in 24 Bollywood films. Kishan claims that spending nearly all his life on film sets has allowed him to learn about the many aspects of film-making. He must have had excellent teachers because the end result is a very special film debut.

Care of Footpath is about an orphan slum boy who sells newspapers on the streets. One day, a group of school children call him an 'uneducated brute'; an insult that drives him to prove them wrong. Eventually, against all odds, he gains a top education and changes attitudes towards slum children.

Kishan has dedicated his film to 'all underprivileged children on this Earth' in the hope that it will inspire them. He wants these children to realise that nothing should stop them from making a better life for themselves.

On 27 March 2006, Kishan was awarded the Guinness World Record for the youngest director of a professionally made feature-length film.

8

ON YOUR MARKS

a. In what three ways was Kishan involved in the film?
b. Why do you think Kishan wanted to be a film director?
c. What do you think 'against all odds' means?
d. Would you want to see the film? Give reasons.

GET SET

a. What did some of the film community think Kishan's film was going to be like?
b. Why would the school children call the boy an 'uneducated brute'?
c. What 'aspects of film-making' do you think Kishan needed to learn to make a film?
d. Do you think underprivileged children would take notice of what Kishan says? Give reasons.

GO FOR GOLD!

a. Write down two phrases that the reviewer uses to describe the film.
b. How do you think the orphan boy could have changed attitudes towards slum children?
c. What does 'technically stunning' mean?
d. What do you admire about Kishan? Why?

BEYOND THE RECORD

Write a plan for a short film that will inspire underprivileged children to find a better life. Where does your film take place? Who is your main character? What happens? Present your ideas to the class.

MOST TATTOOED PERSON

28 Oak Crescent
New Town
South Wales 1111
Australia

10 August 2011

Hi Aisha

How are you? I'm having a great time staying with my gran and granddad.
I hadn't seen them for three years, so we've had a lot of catching up to do.

We've visited loads of places but the best day, without a doubt, was going to a
local arts festival and seeing Lucky Diamond Rich, who holds the Guinness World
Record for the most tattooed person.

He was brilliant, especially when he juggled swords and chainsaws while sitting on
top of a tall unicycle. Mum wouldn't watch but I couldn't take my eyes off him; his
whole body and bald head were totally covered in tattoos!

At the end of his act, Lucky showed the crowd his tattoos, which were kind of inky
bluey-black with swirly patterns, pictures and words tattooed in white on top. Even
his eyelids, gums, ears and the thin skin between his toes were tattooed. He looked
incredible!

When Mum said that it looked painful, Lucky laughed. By the way, all his teeth are silver!

Later, I found out that as a kid he stuck temporary tattoos onto his skin but it
wasn't until he was 17 that he got his first permanent one. He liked the way it
made him look different so he got more and hasn't stopped since.

Lucky is so cool. He doesn't seem to be worried about what people think about him.

Gotta go now. See you soon.

Love Maya

P.S. I have attached a couple of photos so that you can see what Lucky looks like!

ON YOUR MARKS

a. Where did Maya see Lucky Diamond Rich?
b. What do you think Maya's mum thinks about Lucky's juggling act?
c. How can you tell this is an informal letter?
d. How would you feel if you met Lucky Diamond Rich? Why?

GET SET

a. Find and write down two informal phrases used in the letter.
b. Why has Lucky Diamond Rich started to use white tattoos?
c. Why do you think Lucky is not 'worried about what people think about him'?
d. Choose three of your own words to describe Lucky. Give reasons for your choice.

GO FOR GOLD!

a. What did Maya notice when Lucky Diamond Rich laughed?
b. Why might Maya have chosen to write a letter instead of a short postcard?
c. Why do you think Lucky performs at arts festivals?
d. Why do you think people choose to have tattoos?

BEYOND THE RECORD

Choose two sources to help you research and create a short biography about the life of Lucky Diamond Rich. Include an opening introductory paragraph, information about his life and a closing paragraph summarising what you think of him.

LONGEST THEATRICAL RUN

www.sightseeinginlondon.com/theatre/mousetrap

HOME ◆ MUSEUMS ◆ THEATRES ◆ SHOPPING ◆ PARKS

THEATRES
- ◆ Musicals
- ◆ Comedy
- ◆ Drama
- ◆ Calendar
- ◆ Venues

The Mousetrap
St Martin's Theatre, London

Background

On 30 May 1947, a short murder mystery play, written by the great crime writer Dame Agatha Christie, was broadcast on the radio. The name of the play was *Three Blind Mice*.

Five years later, on 25 November 1952, an adapted version for the stage, renamed *The Mousetrap*, opened at the Ambassadors Theatre in London's West End. Sixty glorious years on, it is still going strong and has become one of the most legendary and record-breaking plays of all time.

For many years *The Mousetrap* has held the Guinness World Record for the world's longest theatre run. As of 25 November 2012, an astonishing 25,007 continuous performances have been staged at the Ambassadors Theatre and later at St Martin's Theatre, Cambridge Circus. The production is now in its diamond anniversary year.

The Mousetrap also boasts two further records. David Raven is the most durable West End actor after playing Major Metcalf for 4,575 performances over 11 years and Nancy Seabrooke is the world's longest-serving understudy for 6,240 performances over 15 years.

The plot

Set in a small country hotel, cut off by snow, the owners and their various guests are shocked when one of them is found dead. Experience the suspense as the elaborate plot, typical of a good Agatha Christie thriller, unravels to finally reveal the identity of the murderer.

As is tradition with the play, theatregoers are asked not to reveal the name of the murderer to those who have not yet seen the production.

ON YOUR MARKS

a. What was the name of the theatre in which *The Mousetrap* was first staged?
b. Why are theatregoers asked not to reveal the identity of the murderer?
c. What does an understudy do?
d. Does the plot make you want to see the play? Give reasons.

GET SET

a. What three Guinness World Records are mentioned in the web page?
b. How many years does a diamond anniversary celebrate?
c. Why is the plot summary so short?
d. Why do you think David Raven played Major Metcalf for so long?

GO FOR GOLD!

a. What adjective is used to mean 'famous'?
b. Why would the radio play need adapting for the stage?
c. In the play, why do you think the country hotel is cut off by snow?
d. What information do you think is missing from the web page?

BEYOND THE RECORD

Use at least two sources to help you to write a short biography of Dame Agatha Christie that could be published in a theatre programme for *The Mousetrap*.

MOST POTS THROWN IN ONE HOUR BY AN INDIVIDUAL

Focus on

Pottery

In pottery terms, to 'throw a pot' literally means to throw a lump of clay onto a pottery wheel and mould it to create a pot. It takes skill and patience; two qualities that record-breaking potter Mark Byles has in abundance.

On 29 June 2009, Mark threw an extraordinary 150 perfect flowerpots in one hour, breaking the Guinness World Record for most pots thrown in one hour by an individual. He achieved this at a thrilling pot-throwing competition held at the Ceramics South East Potters Market at the Friars, Aylesford, UK.

At the end of the competition, a pottery expert carefully measured and checked the rows and rows of flowerpots before announcing Mark as the new Guinness World Record holder.

Try it yourself!

Do you think you could break this record? You'll need to follow strict guidelines provided by Guinness World Records:

- All the pots must be thrown using clay, water, shaping tools, a wheel and hands.
- Each pot must be a flowerpot – wide at the top with a thick rim, and it should be as tall as it is wide.
- Every pot must look the same.
- A lump of clay that weighs no less that 600 g must be used.
- The height and diameter of the pot must measure between 11.5 cm and 14 cm.

Arts & Crafts *September 2009*   23

ON YOUR MARKS

a. What kind of pots did Mark Byles 'throw' to break the record?
b. Why do you think the competition might have been 'thrilling'?
c. Why are the guidelines in a bulleted list?
d. Do you think it was a difficult record to break? Why?

GET SET

a. Write down two adjectives that describe Mark Byles' flowerpots.
b. Why do you think there are strict guidelines for this Guinness World Record?
c. How do you think the writer feels about Mark's pottery skills?
d. Would this magazine article make you want to try 'throwing' a pot? Why?

GO FOR GOLD!

a. What other word is used in the text which means 'pottery'?
b. Why do you think the guidelines insist on flowerpots for record attempts?
c. Why was a pottery expert needed to check the finished flowerpots?
d. Which guideline do you think would be most difficult to adhere to? Why?

BEYOND THE RECORD

Use printed and internet sources to help you create an instruction text on 'How to throw a clay pot' for people keen to learn how to do it. Think about how you will lay out the instructions and information so that the text is easy to follow, for example using bulleted lists, labelled diagrams and instructional language.

LONGEST RAIL GRIND ON A SNOWBOARD

INDOOR SNOWBOARDING TRIUMPH!

British snowboarder, Calum Paton, 14, has become a snowboarding star after breaking the Guinness World Record for the longest rail grind on a snowboard. He rode an incredible 78.7 m down the rail.

The record-breaking rail grind event took place on 2 December, and was organised specifically to give UK snowboarders the chance to try to break the existing world record.

On the day itself, UK professional and amateur indoor snowboarders arrived at the Milton Keynes Xscape to attempt the challenge on a custom-built rail that was 91.5 m long. During the five-hour session, snowboarder after snowboarder attempted a record-breaking rail grind ride but, frustratingly, all of them fell short of the record.

What happened next will go down in indoor snowboarding history! With just 10 minutes to go before the end of the event, many enthusiasts had already started packing up to leave. There was only one snowboarder left: young Calum Paton.

On the signal, Calum jumped onto the rail and confidently manoeuvred his board in a 50-50 grind with such balance and control that it seemed as if he was locked onto the rail. As he smoothly slid past the record mark, Calum was hailed as the new Guinness World Record holder.

The organisers say that the event highlights how the UK has some world-class rail riders and a flourishing indoor snowboard scene. As for the hero of the day, he's totally stoked!

Snow and Ice | January 2012

42

YR 6

ON YOUR MARKS

a. Why was the rail grind event in Milton Keynes organised?
b. What do you think 'as if he was locked onto the rail' means?
c. Why do you think the event was held indoors?
d. Do you agree that Calum was 'the hero of the day'? Why?

GET SET

a. How did Calum 'manoeuvre' his snowboard on the rail?
b. Why do you think the rail had to be custom built?
c. Why do you think some people were packing up before the end of the event?
d. Why do you think indoor snowboarding is flourishing in the UK?

GO FOR GOLD!

a. Why were attempts to break the world record 'frustrating'?
b. Calum was 'totally stoked' about breaking the record. What do you think this means?
c. How do you know that this article is meant for snowboard enthusiasts?
d. Why do you think Calum succeeded in breaking the record when others failed?

BEYOND THE RECORD

Use books and the internet to help you compile a 10-term glossary of snowboard moves and tricks. Consider the layout. Think about using sub-headings, easy-to-read captions, diagrams and pictures.

29

HOME / NEWS / **PROFILE** / EVENTS / USEFUL LINKS / CONTACT

Mário Trindade

Mário was born in Vila Real, Portugal, on 25 May 1975. When he was a baby, he was diagnosed with a condition called scoliosis, which causes a curve in the spine. Throughout most of his childhood, Mário undertook special walking exercises and wore a corset in an effort to straighten his spine. Unfortunately, neither of these treatments helped. His only hope was an operation when he was older.

Finally, at 17 years old, Mário underwent surgery to try to correct the problem. Sadly the operation was unsuccessful and, worse still, Mário could not move his legs afterwards.

After a frustrating year of trying to walk again, he was given the hardest decision of his life: to stay in a wheelchair forever or to hope for a miracle in another operation. He chose the wheelchair.

Sometime later, Mário became a member of a disabled basketball team; a decision that turned out to be life changing. As the team became more successful, Mário discovered a new focus for his life – sport.

Since 2001, Mário has competed successfully in wheelchair road and track racing events and marathons using an adapted racing wheelchair.

On 3–4 December 2007, Mário raised awareness of disability in sport by breaking the Guinness World Record for the greatest distance travelled in a wheelchair at the Vila Real Stadium in Vila Real, Portugal. He travelled 182.4 km over two days.

Today, Mário represents Portugal in worldwide athletic events, including the Paralympics. He is an inspiration to disabled and non-disabled people alike for his determination, commitment and courage.

ON YOUR MARKS

a. What is scoliosis?
b. What does 'miracle' mean?
c. What type of text is this? How do you know?
d. Why do you think Mário has so much determination to succeed?

GET SET

a. What adjective is used to describe Mário's operation?
b. How do you think playing basketball helped Mário?
c. Why do you think Mário 'chose' the wheelchair instead of another operation?
d. How do you think Mário's world record helped raise awareness of disability in sport?

GO FOR GOLD!

a. What three inspirational qualities does Mário have?
b. Why do you think the two choices after his operation gave him 'the hardest decision of his life'?
c. Why do you think Mário uses an adapted racing wheelchair?
d. Why do you think Mário wanted to raise awareness of disability in sport?

BEYOND THE RECORD

Mário Trindade started his world record attempt on 3 December 2007, the International Day of People with Disabilities. He did this to show what disabled athletes can do and achieve. Use two sources to research three different sports of the Paralympics. Create a poster for one of the events and use persuasive text to encourage people to come and support it.

26

Kolkata Times Monday 30 January 2012

WORLD RECORD FOR GANDHI PEACE MARCH

Yesterday, 485 under-privileged children, aged between 10 and 16, took part in a half-kilometre peace march through the centre of Kolkata. They were walking in remembrance of one of India's greatest spiritual leaders, Mohandas Gandhi, who was tragically assassinated on that date, 64 years ago.

The marching youngsters also successfully broke the Guinness World Record for the largest gathering of people dressed as Mohandas Gandhi.

Usha Gokani, Gandhi's granddaughter, was among the watching crowds as hundreds of Mohandas Gandhis, wearing identical grey moustaches, round glasses, white traditional Indian dhotis and shawls, walked together as part of the 'Rise Up' peace march. The children carried Gandhi's trademark walking stick and wore skin-coloured caps on their heads.

The idea for the 'Rise Up' peace march came from a small charity called TRACKS (Training Resources and Care For Kids). The charity helps single mothers and children who live in the train stations and streets of Mumbai by providing much-needed health care and advice. Before the event, charity workers taught the children about Gandhi so they could learn more about how he wanted to improve the lives of Indian people through peaceful actions.

by **ADITA DUTTA**

ON YOUR MARKS

a. How old were the children who dressed up as Mohandas Gandhi?
b. Give two reasons why the children would remember 29 January.
c. What do you think a dhoti is?
d. Does the headline make you want to know more? Why?

GET SET

a. How does the reporter describe Mohandas Gandhi?
b. What features tell us this is a news report?
c. What do you think 'Gandhi's trademark walking stick' means?
d. Do you think the record attempt was a good way of honouring Mohandas Gandhi? Why?

GO FOR GOLD!

a. List the five 'W' questions that the report answers (i.e. What? Where? Who? When? Why?).
b. Why did the children wear skin-coloured caps on their heads?
c. What does 'tragic' mean?
d. How do you think the teachings of Gandhi might help under-privileged children?

BEYOND THE RECORD

Use three different sources to find out about the life of Mohandas Gandhi. Use the information to create a short biography of no more than 100 words.

33

COLUMBUS ZOO AND AQUARIUM

POWELL, OHIO, USA

Originally known as Columbus Zoological Gardens, the zoo opened in 1927. It is divided up into different zones, each of which is dedicated to a different region of the world, including North America, Shoreline, African Forest, Asia and Australia.

POWELL, OHIO

Colo the gorilla

The female gorilla, Colo, has lived at the zoo all her life. Colo is a Western Lowland gorilla, and was born on 22 December 1956. Incredibly, Colo holds two Guinness World Records: she is the first ever gorilla born in captivity and, at the age of 55 years, 11 months, 9 days as of 30 November 2012, she is the oldest living gorilla in captivity. Colo has successfully bred a large gorilla family; the zoo currently houses 15 gorillas, six of which are related to Colo.

Colo the gorilla

Conservation

The Columbus Zoo and Aquarium runs a conservation programme that helps to support conservation projects throughout the world. The programme has raised over $4 million in the last five years, to support 70 projects in at least 30 countries worldwide. You can find out more about endangered species during your visit by reading the information provided with the exhibits. Donation boxes are also provided throughout the zoo.

Tips for your trip

The zoo is home to more than 700 species. If your trip is short, make sure you don't miss the Asian elephants, hawksbill sea turtles, red river hogs and Queensland koalas!

Travel Guide to the USA   37

YR 6

ON YOUR MARKS

a. Where was Colo born?
b. Why might the zoo have donation boxes?
c. In which zone do you think you would find the Queensland koalas?
d. What would you like to see if you visited Columbus Zoo and Aquarium? Why?

GET SET

a. How could you find out more about endangered species during your visit?
b. Why is it 'incredible' that Colo holds two Guinness World Records?
c. What does 'captivity' mean?
d. What information do you think is missing from this travel guide page?

GO FOR GOLD!

a. How many of the zoo's gorillas are related to Colo?
b. What does 'endangered' mean?
c. Why has Colo been so important to Columbus Zoo?
d. Do you think it is important that Columbus Zoo has a conservation programme? Why?

BEYOND THE RECORD

Use two sources to find out more about the life of Colo the gorilla and use the information to help you write a biography about her. Consider using photographs or a timeline.

LARGEST MATCHSTICK MODEL

Focus on

Building matchstick models

David Reynolds has a hobby that requires skill, time and a great deal of patience; he builds large-scale matchstick models. In 1994, Mr Reynolds, a retired oil rig engineer, began the painstaking process of creating a matchstick model of a North Sea oil platform.

When it was finally finished in July 2009, the 1,000-kg model, made from 4.075 million matchsticks, measured 3.6 m tall and 6.4 m long. It broke the Guinness World Record for the largest matchstick model/structure/sculpture. Soon after its completion, the model was relocated from the Reynolds' home in Southampton to a local museum.

Matchstick models were first made by prisoners of war over 200 years ago. Today, matchstick modelling has become a popular hobby, with the original fire-lighting matches being replaced by craft matches with blunt ends.

Try it yourself!

The best way to start building matchstick models is to buy a craft kit. Once you have mastered the basics, you can gradually move on to more challenging models, such as David Reynolds' most recent matchstick model of the doomed ship, *Titanic*, made from 120,000 matchsticks.

To get started, you will need:

- a model design
- pre-cut cardboard shapes
- a small paintbrush
- strong glue
- craft matchsticks
- a sharp knife or matchstick cutter
- a cutting board and sandpaper.

Tips for success

- Cut matchsticks to the right size or shape, using a sharp knife or matchstick cutter, before you start to glue them.
- Always use a paintbrush to apply glue, and be sparing with the amount you use.
- 'Clad' pre-cut cardboard shapes with matchsticks. This will give your structure more support.
- To create curved sections, soak the matches in water overnight to make them easier to bend.

ON YOUR MARKS

a. How many matchsticks were used to make the largest matchstick model/structure/sculpture?
b. Why do you think David Reynolds made a model of a North Sea oil platform?
c. Why should you be 'sparing' with the amount of glue you use?
d. Why do you think matchstick modelling is a 'popular hobby'?

GET SET

a. Write down the instruction that explains how to make matches bend.
b. What does the writer mean by 'mastered the basics'?
c. Why do you think the record-breaking model had to be moved out of the Reynolds' house?
d. Which part of the text would you like more information about? Give reasons.

GO FOR GOLD!

a. Write down two examples of imperative verbs used in the tips for success.
b. Why does matchstick modelling need 'a great deal of patience'?
c. Why might a matchstick model structure need more support?
d. Why do you think prisoners of war made matchstick models?

BEYOND THE RECORD

Use books and the internet to search for four different matchstick models. Note down the key information about them. Use this information to create a page from a museum guide. What kind of information might a visitor to the museum want to know?

LARGEST VIOLIN

www.encyclopedia-file.com/largest-violin

Vogtland – a musical place

Vogtland is a region of Germany that is famous for the production of musical instruments such as violins, zithers, French horns, harmonicas and guitars.

Markneukirchen in Vogtland is particularly famous for its violin and bow makers. The first ever German guild for violin makers was created here in 1677 by 12 highly skilled violin and bow makers (masters), and it is now the oldest existing violin-making guild in Germany.

World's largest violin

The world's largest violin was made in Markneukirchen, Germany and is 4.27 m long and 1.4 m wide. It is seven times larger than a normal-sized violin and requires three people to play it: two to move the 5.2-m-long bow and one to press on the violin strings.

This remarkable violin was completed on 14 June 2011 by 15 Vogtland masters of violin and bow making.

The oversized replica was based on a late-18th-century violin made by one of Markneukirchen's most famous violin makers, Johann Georg Schönfelder II.

The world's largest violin is seven times larger than a normal-sized violin.

Johann Georg Schönfelder II

Johann Georg Schönfelder II (1750–1824) was a highly skilled violin maker and a talented musician. His exquisite golden-coloured violins were very popular at the time he made them and continue to be popular now.

ON YOUR MARKS

a. How many people are needed to play the world's largest violin?
b. Why are two people needed to move the bow of the world's largest violin?
c. Why is Vogtland called 'a musical place'?
d. Which part of the largest violin would you have liked to make? Why?

GET SET

a. What two things was Johann Georg Schönfelder II famous for?
b. Why do you think his violins are still popular?
c. What does '(1750–1824)' mean? Why are the numbers in brackets?
d. Which part of this non-chronological report did you find the most interesting? Why?

GO FOR GOLD!

a. How are Johann Georg Schönfelder II's violins described in the text?
b. Why do you think violin and bow makers would want to live and work in Markneukirchen?
c. What does the word 'exquisite' mean?
d. Musical-instrument makers have to train for many years before they can become masters. Why do you think this is?

BEYOND THE RECORD

Use the internet to help you find out more information about Vogtland and Markneukirchen. Use the information to create a page from a travel brochure to persuade visitors to visit the region. Highlight the musical connections and history. Think about the layout and persuasive language you will use.

LARGEST CONCENTRATION OF GEYSERS

Our World Encyclopedia

Geysers

Water

A geyser is a hot water spring that intermittently erupts, and spouts boiling hot water and steam high into the air.

The word **'geyser'** comes from the Icelandic verb **'geysa'** meaning **'to gush'**.

Geysers are only found in Russia, Iceland, Chile, New Zealand and the USA. This is because a combination of three important elements is needed to create a geyser. The three elements are:

- a large amount of water
- a source of heat from an active volcanic area
- an underground plumbing system.

The rarity of these three elements means there are only around 700 known geysers in the world. Yellowstone National Park, which lies mostly within the borders of Wyoming, USA, has at least 300 geysers (up to 250 are active) and holds the Guinness World Record for the largest concentration of geysers.

Each year, thousands of tourists and geyser enthusiasts flock to Yellowstone to watch the geysers.

Well-known Yellowstone National Park geysers

- **Old Faithful** blasts gallons of water up to 55 m in the air every hour.
- **Riverside** spouts water across the Firehole River, creating a rainbow.
- **Great Fountain** shoots water in lots of different directions.
- **Steamboat** is the world's tallest geyser, blasting water up to 121 m high.

How geysers work

1. Rainwater and snow seep into the ground and meet rock heated by volcanic magma.
2. The heated water rises up through channels in the rock. (The rock channels are very tight, stopping the water rising easily to the surface. The channels are known as the 'plumbing system'.)
3. Gradually the plumbing system fills up with hot water.
4. The intense pressure generated by the super-heated water leads to the production of steam.
5. The steam forces the hot water upwards until it is ejected out of the mouth of the geyser.
6. After the geyser has erupted, the process starts again.

18

ON YOUR MARKS

a. Where is Yellowstone National Park?

b. What does 'super-heated' mean?

c. Why is the list in the 'How geysers work' section numbered?

d. Which of the four geysers listed in the text would you like to see? Why?

GET SET

a. What is a 'plumbing system' for a geyser?

b. Why do you think geysers are always found in active volcanic areas?

c. Why might tourists 'flock to Yellowstone to watch the geysers'?

d. What piece of information in the text did you find the most interesting? Why?

GO FOR GOLD!

a. What word in the text means 'uncommon' or 'unusual'?

b. Why do you think 'a large amount of water' is needed to create a geyser?

c. Why do you think geysers are given specific names?

d. What could you add to the text to make it easier for readers to understand how a geyser works? Explain why you would do this.

BEYOND THE RECORD

Use two sources to find out more about the geysers at Yellowstone National Park. Create a presentation about one of the geysers to show to your class. Think about the use of clear, labelled diagrams, pictures, facts or film clips.

LARGEST PHOTO MOSAIC

www.kidscorner123.com/Getinvolved/GuinnessWorldRecords

Kids' corner Learn and have fun!

What's on | Watch | Learn | Games | Contact

A B C D E F **G** H I J K L M N O P Q R S T U V W X Y Z

GUINNESS WORLD RECORDS DAY!

Do you have an idea for a new Guinness World Record or want to try to break one that already exists? Every year, on Guinness World Records (GWR) Day, people from all over the world attempt to set new records or break existing ones. If you want to give it a go, send an application to the GWR website. If all goes well, a GWR adjudicator will check that the record attempt is done properly. Once the record has been attempted, a final decision is made about whether it is a new world record.

The eighth GWR Day was on Thursday, 15 November 2012. Over 420,000 people took part and broke many memorable records, such as the largest chocolate coin in Bologna, Italy, and the most people crammed in a Mini, achieved in London, UK.

On the seventh GWR Day, held on 17 November 2011, one of the most imaginative record attempts was the world's largest photo mosaic. Made on 16 November 2011, in Nagoya, Aichi, Japan, it measured 1,562,39 m². The mosaic was made up of 137,200 photographs of people's pets that, when put together, showed a huge picture of a cat and dog.

Why use photographs of pets, and where did they all come from? The answer? The team who created the mosaic all worked for the Japanese pet store, Smile-one Taichi Matsumto.

ON YOUR MARKS

a. What happens on Guinness World Records Day?

b. Why do you think so many people want to attempt a Guinness World Record?

c. What is the paragraph starting 'Do you have an idea' about?

d. What theme would you choose for a photo mosaic? Why?

GET SET

a. What happened in Bologna, Italy on 15 November 2012?

b. What does 'adjudicator' mean?

c. Why does a Guinness World Records adjudicator need to check that a record attempt is 'done properly'?

d. Do you agree that the photo mosaic record attempt was 'imaginative'? Why?

GO FOR GOLD!

a. Why was the photo mosaic made from photographs of pets?

b. Why do you think some of the records are described as 'memorable'?

c. Why do you think the opening sentence is a question?

d. What record would you attempt to break or set on Guinness World Records Day? Why?

BEYOND THE RECORD

Use the Guinness World Records website to select your favourite three records. Create a PowerPoint® presentation explaining what they are. Share your presentation with others in your class and discuss why you chose the three records.

News October 2007

A FOOT-FLIPPING FEAT

GYMNASTICS UK NEWSLETTER

On Wednesday, 19 September, Hou Yanan and Jiang Tiantian from the Chinese Wuqiao County Aerobatic Group performed a remarkable feat that propelled them into the Guinness World Records archives.

The two acrobats were invited to appear on the set of the TV programme *Zheng Da Zong Yi* in Beijing, China, to attempt to break the Guinness World Record for most consecutive foot-juggling flips.

With judges looking on, the first acrobat lay back on a sloped padded stool and held her legs straight up in the air. The second acrobat then lay facing downwards on the first acrobat's legs, balancing on her stomach.

With incredible accuracy, the first acrobat bent her legs and pushed the other acrobat into the air to perform a full somersault. With precise rhythm, the two acrobats repeated this action to achieve an incredible 90 foot-juggling flips.

Hou Yanan and Jiang Tiantian's achievement is yet another example of the remarkable skill and discipline displayed by Chinese acrobats. Many come from Wuqiao County, in the North China Plain, which is famous for producing the best acrobats in China. Pupils start training as young as the age of five and each acrobatic move is practised over and over again until it is perfect.

4

ON YOUR MARKS

a. What group do Hou and Jiang belong to?
b. Why were judges 'looking on'?
c. How would a 'sloped padded stool' help the acrobats?
d. Do you think the two acrobats were 'remarkable'? Why?

GET SET

a. What is Wuqiao County famous for?
b. Why do pupils at Chinese acrobatic schools start training when they are young?
c. What do you notice about the title of the article? Why has the writer chosen to use these words?
d. Write down one good point and one bad point about having to practise something over and over again.

GO FOR GOLD!

a. Write down the two qualities that Chinese acrobats have.
b. How does the writer give the impression that acrobats are great?
c. Why has the writer used the words 'feat' and 'propelled' in the first paragraph?
d. What kind of training do you think the two acrobats did to prepare for this record attempt?

BEYOND THE RECORD

Imagine you are interviewing Hou Yanan and Jiang Tiantian after their record attempt. Write down five questions that you would like to ask them about the record attempt and how they prepared for it. Role-play the interview, taking it in turns to ask your questions to the 'acrobats'.

Focus on

Painting panoramas

Panoramic paintings are huge artworks that show a full view of something such as a landscape, a city, a battle or an event. They can take many months, even years, of work with several artists painting different sections of the view at the same time. Panoramic painting techniques were particularly popular in the mid-19th century, and were created to show landscapes or historical events.

On 26 April 2011, a panoramic painting called 'Splendid Central Plains' was unveiled by the Henan Administration of Radio Film and Television (China) at the Tower of Fortune in Zhengzhou City, Henan Province, China.

Working on a 163.52-m-long and 18.422-m-wide canvas, 13 painters took 345 days to paint a panoramic view of the landscapes and landmarks of the Henan province. The finished panoramic painting measured 3,012.365 m² (nearly 2 miles!), breaking the Guinness World Record for largest panoramic painting.

Try it yourself!

Would you like to recreate your favourite view using the panoramic painting technique? *Arts & Crafts* magazine shows you how …

1 Start by slowly scanning your chosen view, from left to right. What you're seeing is a panorama. Break up the view into three or four sections.
2 Next, use a notebook to make sketches (or you may prefer to take photographs) of the different sections of your panorama.
3 Divide a long piece of paper into sections. You are now ready to paint. Make sure you have your sketches, or photos, nearby.
4 Begin by painting the background (sky, fields, etc.).
5 After that, paint in the middle ground for each section (buildings, fences, ponds).
6 Finally, add in the detailed foreground (livestock, plants, gates).

ON YOUR MARKS

a. What was the name of the record-breaking panoramic painting?

b. Why were 13 painters needed to paint the largest panoramic painting?

c. If you were using the panoramic painting technique, why would you need to make sketches or take photographs of the view?

d. Would you take photos or make sketches for step 2? Why?

GET SET

a. What are the measurements of the world's largest panoramic painting?

b. What does 'panoramic' mean?

c. Why are the instructions in the text numbered?

d. Why do you think panoramic paintings were very popular in the 19th century?

GO FOR GOLD!

a. Write down two time connectives used in the text.

b. Why do you need to begin a panoramic painting by 'slowly scanning your chosen view'?

c. Why do you think people from the Henan Province would want to see the largest panoramic painting?

d. Would you prefer to create a panoramic school painting on your own or with a team of others? Give reasons.

BEYOND THE RECORD

Use the internet and art books to study some examples of panoramic paintings and photographs. Choose one panoramic painting or photograph and write interesting information about it for visitors to an art exhibition. How can you make the visitors look more closely at the picture?

AN INCREDIBLE LIFE STORY
William Lawlis Pace

Liz Ellis looks back on Pace's incredible life.

William Lawlis Pace was born on 27 February 1909 in Wheeler, Texas, USA to a poor farming family. In October 1917, when he was eight years old, Pace was accidentally shot in the head by his older brother while they were playing with their father's 22-calibre rifle. Neither of the boys had thought that the gun was loaded.

The bullet permanently damaged Pace's right eye, his ear and facial nerves, causing his face to pull up to one side. The doctors at the hospital in Dallas decided not to take the bullet out as an operation could cause serious brain damage.

Despite his disabilities, Pace courageously continued to study at school and to actively play baseball as a catcher. Later he became a farmer and in 1933 he married Onetia and went on to have three children.

In the 1940s, Pace and his family moved to California where he became a cemetery caretaker. When he retired, Pace and Onetia travelled the world, visiting countries such as Egypt and Australia until Onetia died in 2004.

At the age of 97, Pace became a celebrity. On 20 July 2006, hospital X-rays confirmed that, 89 years after he was shot, the bullet was still in his head, making him the Guinness World Record holder for the longest time to live with a bullet in the head.

William Pace died on 23 April 2012 at the age of 103, in Turlock, California, USA.

Pace's long life was remarkable. His family believe he survived because of his hard-working and happy nature.

ON YOUR MARKS

a. Where was William Lawlis Pace born?

b. Why was Pace's long life 'remarkable'?

c. Why did Pace need to have an X-ray to confirm the bullet was still in his head?

d. How do you think Pace's brother felt after the accident? Why?

GET SET

a. Why was the bullet not taken out of Pace's head?

b. Why was it brave for Pace to be a catcher in baseball?

c. What type of text is this? How do you know?

d. How has the author given us a good sense of Pace's life?

GO FOR GOLD!

a. Why did William's family believe he survived?

b. Why did the author use the word 'courageously'?

c. Why do you think Pace wanted to carry on as normal after the accident?

d. Would you have liked to meet William Pace? Why?

BEYOND THE RECORD

Choose a famous person from the past. Use the internet to find out more information about them and write three paragraphs to summarise their life. Ask someone else to review your work. Does it sum up their life in an interesting way?

www.bloggingforlife.com/Harveywk12

DEC 4

December 4, 2011 22:16 GMT

*Posted by **Harveywk12***

Kampfire for the King

Hi folks. I'm just on my way back from the *Kampfire for the King* festival in Alabama. I had the most incredible experience while I was there and I felt I had to share it with you all.

My friend, Joe, and I spent a fantastic afternoon listening to some of our favourite bands, eating and generally soaking up the atmosphere of the Christmas fair.

At 6.00 pm, the main event was announced over the tannoy. US stuntman Ted Batchelor, who specialises in stunts involving (yes, you've guessed it) fire, was about to try to break the Guinness World Record for the longest distance running while on fire!

Crowds of people were waiting behind safety barriers on either side of a long track, so Joe and I squeezed through a gap for a hot and fiery view. And we weren't disappointed. At 6.30 pm, Ted appeared in front of the crowds, covered with fuel, and before we knew what was happening an intensely bright ball of fire on legs raced down the track towards us. It was really weird; as Ted got closer, you could see him quite clearly, wrapped in the flames.

By this time the whole place had gone mad – people were cheering and screaming. The noise was deafening. Once he'd reached the end of the track, he turned right round and started running back to the starting line!

After all the cheering had died down, we heard that the awesome 'Man on Fire' had done it – he had run 150.23 m. What a huge achievement.

SAFETY NOTICE
DO NOT TRY THIS AT HOME! Ted is a trained stuntman and has a team of experts to keep him safe.

Search

January

February

March

April

May

June

July

August

September

October

November

December

ON YOUR MARKS

a. What type of stunts does Ted Batchelor perform?
b. What does Harvey mean by 'the whole place had gone mad'?
c. Why would the crowd be screaming?
d. Why do you think Harvey includes a safety notice?

GET SET

a. How did Joe and Harvey get close to see Ted?
b. What does Harvey mean by a 'hot and fiery view'?
c. Why were safety barriers put up?
d. Do you think Harvey manages to convey the excitement of watching this record being broken in his blog? Why, or why not?

GO FOR GOLD!

a. What other name does Harvey call Ted Batchelor?
b. What does Harvey mean by 'soaking up the atmosphere'?
c. Who do you think Harvey's audience is?
d. How do you feel about what Ted Batchelor does? Give reasons.

BEYOND THE RECORD

Imagine that Ted is coming to your school to give a talk about his fire stunts and world records. With a partner, or on your own, write a list of six questions that you would like to ask him. Use these questions in a hot-seating drama activity with a partner.

OLDEST SCULPTURE

www.encyclopedia-file.com/oldest-sculpture

Sculpture

A sculpture is a 3D work of art that can be made from a range of materials using different methods such as carving, modelling and casting.

Early sculptures

Evidence shows that early humans began to carve small sculptures of animals and figures about 40,000 years ago. The pieces were made from stone, bone, horn, wood and ivory tusks from woolly mammoths, and were created using simple, sharp tools. Although any wooden structures have since rotted away, some sculptures made of harder materials have survived, allowing us insights into the ancient way of life.

World's oldest known sculpture

In Siberia, Russia, artefacts that are over 30,000 years old have been found along the banks of the Khilok River near the town of Tolbaga. Among them was a head of a bear carved onto a piece of backbone or vertebra from a prehistoric woolly rhinoceros. Archaeologists have used carbon dating to date this object to about 35,000 years old. This makes the carving the oldest known sculpture, according to Guinness World Records.

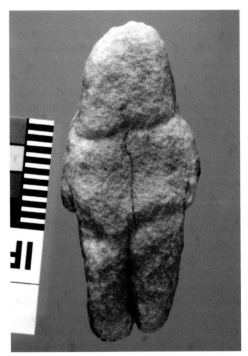

This stone figurine was found in Morocco. Named 'Tan-Tan', it dates back to 400,000 years ago. It is much older than the Tolbaga piece, but is not a sculpture.

Prehistoric sculpture figures

Recently, archaeologists have found some of the world's oldest sculptured human figures, in a group of ancient caves in the German mountains called the Swabian Alps. The main finds came from four caves: the Vogelherd, Hohlenstein-Stadel, Geißenklösterle and Hohle Fels caves. They were all made from woolly mammoth ivory tusks. One of the most famous is a female figure called the Venus of Hohle Fels, who archaeologists have dated to between 35,000 and 40,000 years ago, making her one of the oldest known sculpted figures in the world.

ON YOUR MARKS

a. What is the world's oldest known sculpture?
b. Why do you think most early sculptures were small?
c. What does 'a range of materials' mean?
d. Which hyperlink would you click on? Why?

GET SET

a. Where was the world's oldest sculpture found?
b. Why do you think early sculptures were mostly carved from wood, bone, stone and tusks?
c. What is an 'artefact'?
d. Why do you think no sculptures have been found that are over 40,000 years old?

GO FOR GOLD!

a. Why have no early wooden carvings been found?
b. Why do you think many artefacts have been found in caves and near river banks?
c. Why is it important for archaeologists to carbon-date artefacts?
d. Who do you think is the audience for this web page?

BEYOND THE RECORD

Use two sources to find out more about other sculptures that hold a Guinness World Record, such as the largest chocolate sculpture, the longest sand sculpture, or the largest scrap metal sculpture. Choose your favourite and write down five bullet points to summarise why you like it.

The herbal *Revolution*

Fabia Carbone

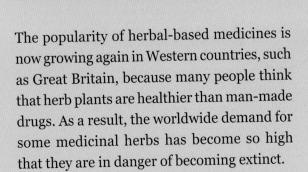

Many of us have eaten liquorice or mint-flavoured sweets, but did you know that both liquorice and mint are herb plants used in medicines? Liquorice can help soothe sore throats and mint can be used to calm indigestion.

In the past, people often used natural herbal medicines when they were unwell. Different parts of herb plants, such as the roots, bark, leaves or flowers, were used to help cure particular ailments.

As time passed, and with the development of new scientific discoveries, many natural remedies were rejected in favour of new medicines produced from man-made chemicals. The exception to this is in China, and other Eastern countries, where a large proportion of the population continue to use traditional medicinal herbs in their everyday medicines and tonics.

The popularity of herbal-based medicines is now growing again in Western countries, such as Great Britain, because many people think that herb plants are healthier than man-made drugs. As a result, the worldwide demand for some medicinal herbs has become so high that they are in danger of becoming extinct.

Luckily, many of these endangered plants are protected in the Guangxi Botanical Garden of Medicinal Plants in Nanning City, Guangxi Province, in China. Within a total area of over 2 km², the garden has 5,600 varieties of medicinal herbs. On 9 December 2011 it was recognised by Guinness World Records as the world's largest medicinal herb garden.

Since it opened, over 50 years ago, the garden staff have saved thousands of medicinal herb plants, stored 3,200 different types of medicinal plant seed and collected approximately 100,000 ancient and modern pictures of medicinal plants. As a result of this special garden, medicinal herb plants have a stronger future as alternative remedies or as a complementary mix with modern medicine.

ON YOUR MARKS

a. What parts of herb plants can be used to create medicines?
b. Why do you think people in the past often took herbal medicines?
c. Why are herb plants seen as healthier than man-made drugs?
d. Which medicines do you think are better: man-made or herbal? Why?

GET SET

a. How many pictures of medicinal plants have the garden staff collected?
b. How does the garden protect the future of medicinal herb plants?
c. How does the author want us to feel about the Guangxi Botanical Garden of Medicinal Plants?
d. What other information do you think could have been added to the text to make it more interesting? Give reasons.

GO FOR GOLD!

a. Write down three connective phrases or words used in the text.
b. Why do you think the world's largest medicinal herb garden is in China?
c. How could ancient and modern pictures of medicinal plants help safeguard their future?
d. Do you think it is a good thing that herbal medicines are in demand again? Give reasons.

BEYOND THE RECORD

Choose two sources to find out about medicinal herbs and flowers that grow in Britain (examples are mint, chickweed and dandelions). Select one plant and make notes on its habitat, what it looks like and what it can be used for.

READING SKILLS

There are different skills you need to learn when reading texts.

Each AF (assessment focus) describes a different set of reading skills. In this book, you will actively practise and improve your ability to do the following.

AF2:

- Find information in a text.
- Find evidence in a text.

AF3:

- Understand what the writer means but does not tell you directly.

AF4:

- Find patterns in a text.
- Comment on organisation of texts.

AF5:

- Understand why the writer chooses a word.
- Understand why writers sometimes use very short sentences.
- Comment on how a writer uses language for effect.

AF6:

- Identify the writer's purpose.
- Understand the writer's viewpoint and the overall effect of the text.